MINISTRY OF MUNITIONS.

Technical Department—Aircraft Production.

I.C. 628.

Kingsway,

W.C. 2.

REPORT ON THE
A.E.G. ARMOURED AEROPLANE

including

D.F.W. GIANT AEROPLANE.

This report is a translation of an article from
Fugsport April 16th. 1919 and is issued as being
of interest.

The Naval & Military Press Ltd

Published by
The Naval & Military Press Ltd
5 Riverside, Brambleside, Bellbrook
Industrial Estate, Uckfield, East Sussex,
TN22 1QQ England

Tel: +44 (0) 1825 749494
Fax: +44 (0) 1825 765701

www.naval-military-press.com
www.military-genealogy.com

MINISTRY OF MUNITIONS.

Technical Department—Aircraft Production.

I.C. 628.

Kingsway,

W.C. 2.

REPORT ON THE
A.E.G. ARMOURED AEROPLANE

JULY, 1918.

REPORT

ON

A.E.G. ARMOURED AEROPLANE.

This machine was brought down by an R.E.8 of 21st Squadron, near Hinges, on May 16, 1918.

It bears the date February 3, 1918, stamped on the main planes, and also on portions of the fuselage, and is the first of its type to have been secured.

This Aeroplane is designed for the purpose of carrying out offensive patrols against infantry, and is furnished with armour, which affords protection for its personnel. This armour appears, however, to be more or less experimental.

In general construction it closely follows the lines of the A.E.G. Twin Engined Bomber G.105, reported on in I.C. 607, though the arrangement of the power plant is, of course, entirely different.

A steel tubular construction is used practically throughout. The machine was badly crashed, and some details are, therefore, not available; but the General Arrangement Drawings at the end of this report may be regarded as substantially accurate.

The leading particulars of the machine are as follows:—

Area of upper wings	190.4 sq. ft.
Area of lower wings	168 sq. ft.
Total area of wings	358.4 sq. ft.
Area of upper aileron	11.2 sq. ft.
Area of lower aileron	10 sq. ft.
Area of tail plane	9.4 sq. ft.
Area of fin	7.6 sq. ft.
Area of rudder	6 sq. ft.
Horizontal area of body	48.6 sq. ft.
Side area of body	54.8 sq. ft.
Cross sectional area of body	14.4 sq. ft.
Area of side armour	33 sq. ft.
Area of bottom armour	29.4 sq. ft.
Area of armour bulkhead	10.4 sq. ft.
Engine, 200 H.P. " Benz "	
Crew—pilot and gunner	360 lbs.
Armament—three guns.	
Petrol capacity	38 gallons
Oil capacity	3 gallons

The principal dimensions are shown on the General Arrangement Drawings.

Construction.

WINGS.

The manner in which the wings are constructed is exactly as shown in the report of the A.E.G. Bomber—i.e., the spars consist of two steel tubes 40 mm. in diameter by .75 mm. thick. At their ends the upper and lower surfaces of the spares are chamfered away, and flat plates welded in position, so as to provide a taper within the washed-out portion of the wing tips. The wings were, unfortunately, so badly damaged that no accurate drawing of their section can be taken, but there is evidence that this very closely follows the section of the bomber, which has already been published. The ribs are of wood, and between each main rib is placed a half-rib joining the front spar to the semi-circular section wooden strip which forms the leading edge. The wing construction is strengthened by two light steel tubes passing through the ribs close behind and parallel to the leading spar, which are used for housing the aileron control wires. The bracing against drag consists of wires and transverse steel tubes welded in position. At the inner end of the wings special reinforced ribs of light gauge steel tube are provided. The method of construction at this point is clearly shown in Fig. 1, which also indicates the manner in which the bracing tube is welded to a socket driven on the main spar. The spars are attached to the fuselage by plain pin joints.

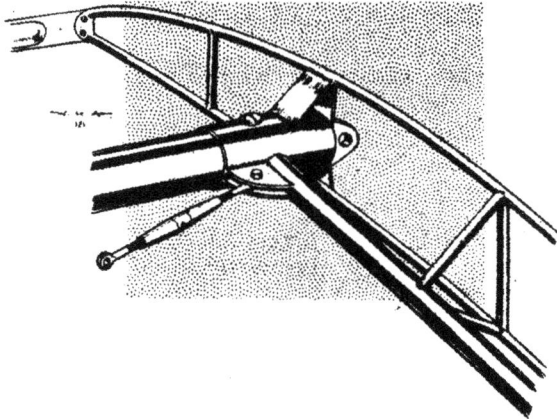

Fig. 1.

CENTRE SECTION.

The centre section of the upper surface is constructed in a similar manner to that of the wings, except that it is considerably reinforced, and the spars are larger in diameter. The leading spar has a diameter of 51 mm. and the rear spar 45 mm. The centre section is secured to the fuselage by a system of stream-lined steel struts, the feet of which terminate in ball-ends dropped into sockets, and there bolted in position. One of these struts is shown in Fig. 2.

The centre section contains an auxiliary gravity petrol tank, and also the radiator, and is, therefore, substantially braced with steel tube transverse members.
The wings are set with a dihedral angle cf approximately 6 deg.

AILERONS.

The aileron framework is of light steel tube throughout, the tube forming the trailing edge being flattened into an eliptical section. The ribs are fixed by welding. The framework of the ailerons on the upper wing is reinforced by diagonal bracing of light tube.

STRUTS.

These are of light steel tube stream-line in section, tapered at each end, and terminating in a socket which abuts against a ball-headed pedestal carried on the win spars; through the socket and the ball is passed a small bolt. The manner in which th attachment is carried out is exactly similar to that described in I.C. 607.

FUSELAGE.

The whole of the fuselage is built up of steel tubes welded together, and having affixed at their junctions sheet steel lugs, which serve as the anchorage for the bracing wires. The diameter of the longerons and of the frame verticals is 20 mm., except the last three members adjacent to the tail, of which the diameter is 16 mm. The welding throughout the fuselage appears to be of very high quality. In Fig. 2 is illustrated a joint, which occurs in the fuselage immediately in front of the pilot's cockpit. The longeron is, from this point to the rear of the gunner's cockpit, fitted with a wooden strip taped in position. This joint shows the method in which the cross bracing wires are furnished with an anchorage. In one or two points in the frame construction the bracing wire lies in the same plane as the transverse tube, and to allow for this a diagonal hole is drilled through the tube, and filled in with a small steel tube welded in place.

Fig. 2.

ENGINE MOUNTING.

This consists of a triangulated arrangement of steel tubes carrying hollow rectangular section steel bearers, on which the crank chamber is slung. The bearers are well trussed both in the vertical and horizontal planes, and are shown in dotted lines in the General Arrangement Drawings. The engine bearers themselves are 2 mm. in thickness, and have an approximate section of $2\frac{1}{16}$ in. by $1\frac{1}{2}$ in.

TAIL.

The empennage possesses no particular points of interest, the planes having the usual steel tubular framework. The tail plane is not fitted with any trimming gear, but a method of adjustment is provided. This is shown in Fig. 3, which is self-explanatory. The diagonal struts which proceed from the base of the fuselage to the tail plane spar are

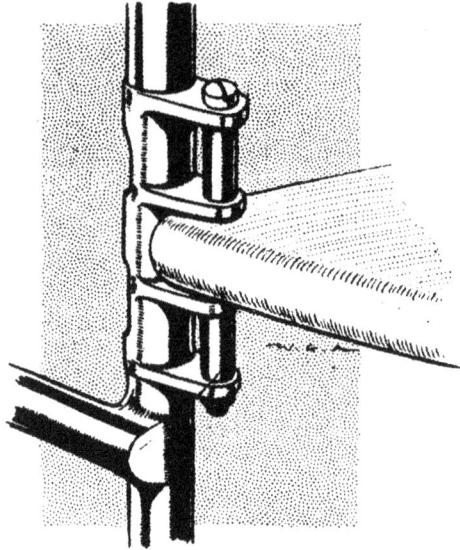

Fig. 3.

fitted at each end with a method of adjustment shown in Fig. 4, allowing them to be extended as required according to the particular socket which is used to carry the leading edge of the tail plane. Neither the elevators nor the rudder are balanced. The rudder post is mounted on the end of the fuselage, as shown in Fig. 5, in which it will be seen that the vertical frame tube of the fin is very stoutly attached to the frame by a triangulated foot.

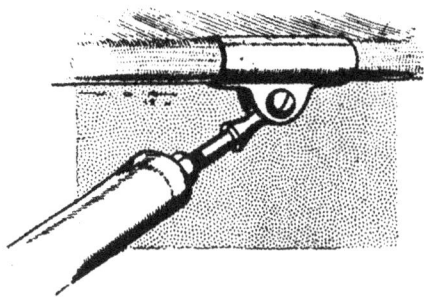

Fig. 4.

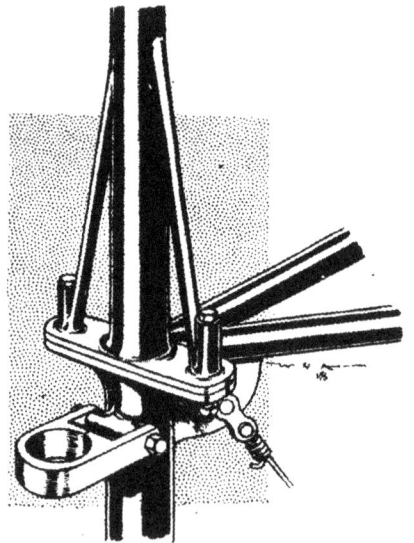

Fig. 5.

LANDING GEAR.

This is of the usual A.E.G. type, and is furnished with shock absorbers consisting of metal coil springs in direct tension, as is clearly shown in the General Arrangement Drawing.

The landing carriage axle has a diameter of 55 mm. The landing carriage struts, which are of similar section to those used between the planes, measure 70 mm. by 37 mm. At their upper ends they are furnished with ball and socket attachments similar to those of the interplane struts.

The wheels are fitted with 810 by 125 mm. tyres, and the track is 6 ft. 10½ in.

The tail skid is unusually heavy, and it is a built-up construction of welded sheet steel. It is mounted on a stout tail post, which is reinforced by four stream-line steel diagonals. The forward end of the tail skid projects inside the fuselage, and is there provided with four steel springs in direct tension. A sketch of the tail skid is given in Fig. 6.

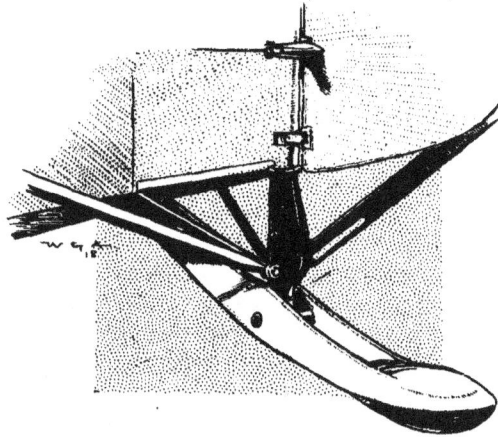

Fig. 6.

CONTROL.

This consists of the usual double-handled lever mounted on a transverse rocking shaft, which carries the elevator control cranks at each end. The upper ailerons are worked positively by wires which pass over pulleys on the wings spars at the outer struts, the outer and lower ailerons being connected by a stream-line steel tubular strut.

ENGINE.

The 200 H.P. Benz engine possesses no new features, and has already been made the subject of an exhaustive report.

PETROL SYSTEM.

Underneath the pilot's seat are the two main petrol tanks, each of which contains 80 litres (equals 16 gallons). These tanks are of brass, and are fitted with Maximall level indicators. The gravity tank, containing 27 litres (equals 5½ gallons) is embedded in the centre section of the upper plane, where it forms the leading edge on the left-hand side. This tank is made of lead-covered steel. Cocks are provided, so that either the gravity tank or the pressure tanks, separately or together, can feed the carburettor.

It is of interest to note that the chamber which is used in connection with the Benz petrol supply system is not, as is usually the case, contained in the main tank, but is a separate fitting mounted on the side of the engine.

RADIATOR.

The radiator is of the Daimler-Mercedes type, measuring 32½ in. long by 11½ in. high and 6 in. deep. This is fitted with imitation honeycomb tubes, of which there are 118 running vertically, each being fitted with 48 gills. The radiator is carried in a steel cradle, into which it is easily inserted from above, and this in turn is supported on specially built-up steel ribs. It is placed so that the tank which forms the upper part of the radiator lies about flush with the centre section of the top plane. The shutter or flap for controlling the water temperature is made of 3-ply wood stiffened with a light steel framework, and is mounted immediately behind the radiator, being worked by a handle within reach of the pilot. This handle is provided with a rack and pawl device. The shutter is 3¾ in. deep, and is capable, therefore, of covering up about one-third of the total radiator surface. It will be noted that the position of the shutter behind the radiator is unusual.

ARMOUR.

Protection for the pilot and gunner is afforded by armour, which is shown in the General Arrangement Drawing in thick lines. There are three panels at each side, and three panels at the bottom of the fuselage, an armour bulkhead being placed at the rear of the gunner's cockpit to protect him from behind. The armour is 5·1 mm. thick, and its total area is 105.8 sq. ft. The weight of the armour is thus approximately 860 lbs.

Careful tests have been made to ascertain the effectiveness of this armour, and the following table gives the ranges at which these plates are safe or unsafe against penetration by bullets of various types. These figures may be taken as correct within the limit of a practical firing test.

Ammunition.	Angle to Normal degrees.	Safe range. yards.	Unsafe range. yards.
German A.P. ...	0	—	600
	15	500	400
	30	400	300
Mark VII. P. {	0 probably	700	600
Armour piercing	15	400	300
	30	300	200
German Spitze ...	0	150	100
	15	100	50
	30	50	
Mark VII.	0	50	
	15	50	
	30	50	

The armour is undoubtedly too light to afford protection against British armour-piercing bullets fired from the ground at a lower height than 500 feet, while a machine armoured with it would have to fly at, at least, 1,000 feet to be safe from all but a very low percentage of hits.

The armour does not appear to have been employed, as it might well have been, in a structural capacity—i.e., it is simply an attachment to the framework, to which it adds no material strength. Its appearance seems to point to the fact that it had been added by way of experiment, and that it was of a more or less makeshift character. It had, for instance, evidently been necessary to open out existing holes and cut new holes in the course of erection. The armour is attached by setscrews to clips clamped on the fuselage members, as shown in Fig. 7.

Fig. 7.

ARMAMENT.

In this machine the pilot is not provided with a gun, but the observer has to control three, of which two (Spandau) are fixed on the flooring of his cockpit, whilst the other (Parabellum) is carried on a rotatable mounting.

With regard to the fixed guns, these are secured to a couple of tubular steel brackets, mounted as shown in Fig. 8. The oval-section steel tubes, of which these brackets are composed, are welded to a light steel base, which forms a sort of tray, and is in turn bolted to the panel of armour which forms the floor of the cockpit.

Adjacent to these two guns, which fire forward at an angle of 45 deg., is a bracket carrying the belts of ammunition, which are fed from a large rotating drum.

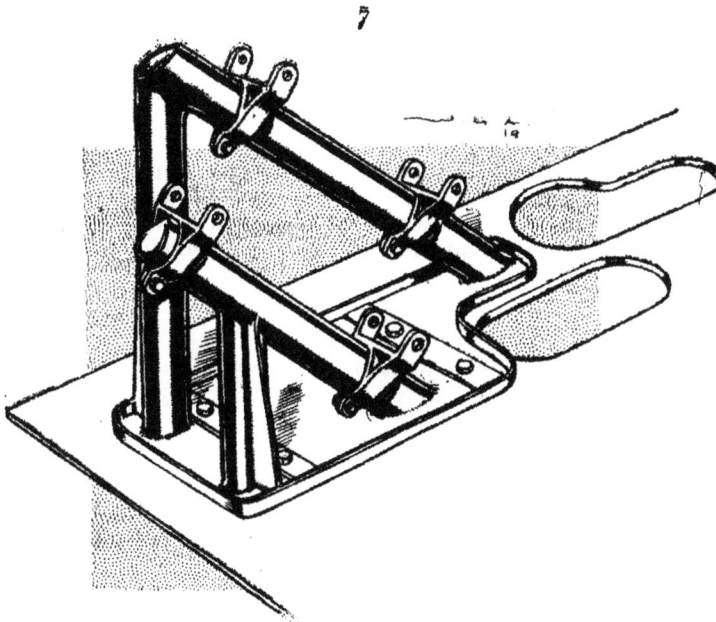

Fig. 8.

In the right-hand front corner of the pilot's cockpit floor is a circular hole, which he would appear to use for sight purposes.

The fixed guns are controlled by Bowden wires and triggers mounted on a diagonal frame member, convenient to the gunner's right hand, as shown in Fig. 9.

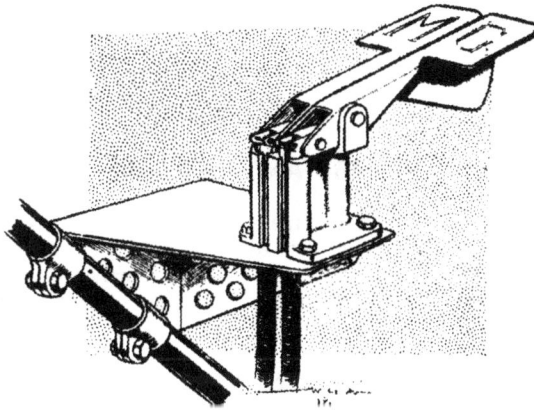

Fig. 9.

The movable gun is of the Parabellum type, and the mounting is of the usual built-up wood variety. The gun cradle is, however, novel, the fixture for this purpose being illustrated in Fig. 10. It appears to be rather more handy than the usual German device, but is by no means lacking in weight. This fitting was in a very badly smashed condition.

The vertical carrier is swivelled at its base, and is secured in position by sliding bolts engaging with teeth cut in the turned-up base plate. These sliding bolts are worked

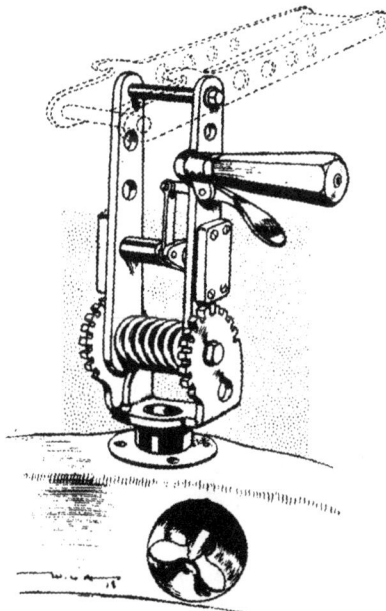

Fig. 10.

b·· a direct acting thumb lever. The turn-table is made of a single hoop of wood reinforced at the point where the gun is mounted by glued-on strips of ply-wood. A locking device of the type shown in Fig. 11 is fitted.

The transverse bracing in the immediate rear of the gunner's cockpit, at which point is mounted the armour bulkhead, suggests that it was the original intention for this aeroplane to carry a gun or guns firing downwards and backwards through a hole in the fuselage. The transverse arrangement of steel tubes and bracing wires is shown in Fig. 12.

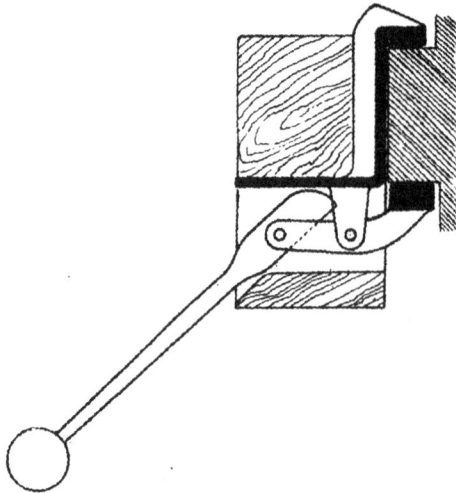

Fig. 11.

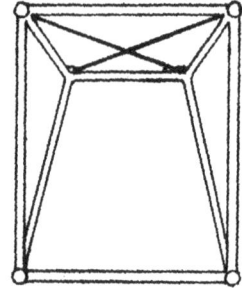

Fig. 12.

WIRELESS AND HEATING.

The machine is fitted with the usual wireless leads and apparatus for heating, the dynamo being carried on a bracket attached to the fuselage immediately in front of the pilot's seat, where it is directly driven from the engine through a hand-controlled clutch. No wireless fittings, other than the dynamo and the leads, were found on the machine.

INSTRUMENTS.

The instruments fitted to this machine are of standard type, and possess no new features of interest.

FABRIC AND DOPE.

The fabric throughout is of good quality, but the dope appears to have been badly applied, as in many points it had completely peeled off the fabric.

CAMOUFLAGE.

The colours used are dark purple and dark green, and in contradistinction to the usual method by which they are arranged in well-defined polygons, are applied so as to give a cloudy effect, and appear to have been sprayed on.

STEEL ANALYSIS.

A sample of the wing spar yields the following analysis:—

Carbon	...	.098 per cent.
Silicon	...	.011 per cent.
Sulphur	...	.017 per cent.
Phosphor	...	.014 per cent.
Manganese	...	.461 per cent.
Chromium	...	.036 per cent.

W.G.A. (Ap.D.L.).

J. G. WEIR,

Lieut.-Colonel,

Controller. Technical Department

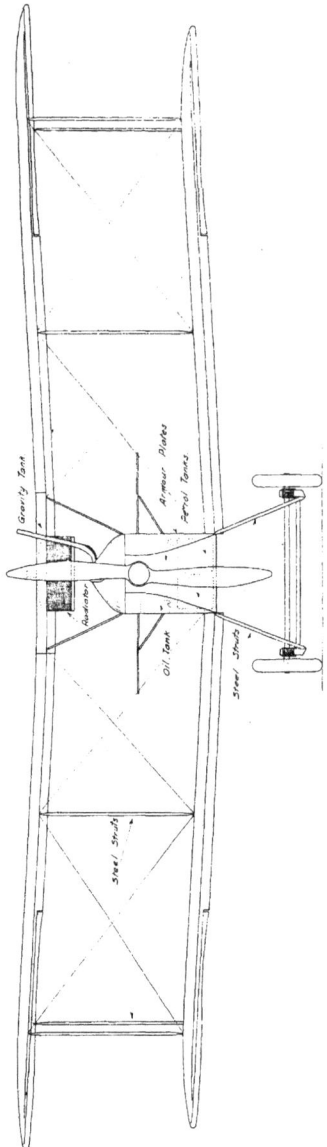

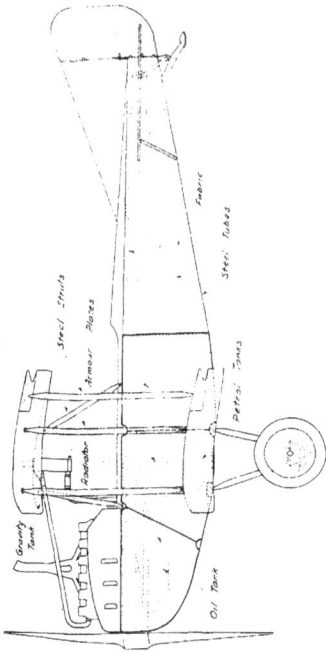

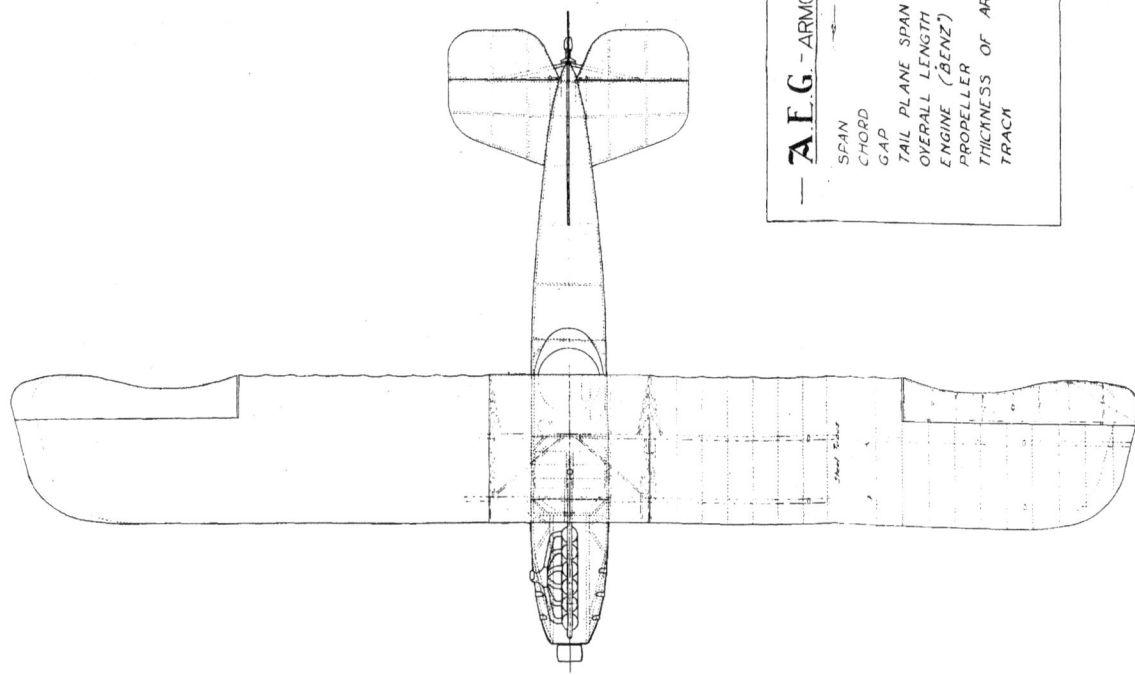

A. E. G. – ARMOURED – AEROPLANE –

SPAN	42' 6"
CHORD	5' 4"
GAP	6' 6"
TAIL PLANE SPAN	9' 0"
OVERALL LENGTH	23' 7"
ENGINE (BENZ")	200 H.P.
PROPELLER	10'-3" DIA.
THICKNESS OF ARMOUR	5 ⁵⁄₁₀
TRACK	6'-10½"

Gravity Tank

Armour Plates

Petrol Tanks

Radiator

Oil Tank

Steel Struts

Steel Struts

Steel Struts

Steel Struts

Armour Plates

Fabric

Steel Tubes

Petrol Tanks

Radiator

Gravity Tank

Oil Tank

Steel Tubes

AIR MINISTRY

DIRECTORATE OF RESEARCH

Central House,
Kingsway, W.C.2.

C 672.

D.F.W. GIANT AEROPLANE.

This report is a translation of an article from
Fugsport April 16th. 1919 and is issued as being
of interest.

H.R. Brooke Popham
       Brigadier General
       Director of Research.

THE DEVELOPMENT OF D.F.W.GIANT AEROPLANES.

      The construction of the first giant machine, D.F.W. **R.I.** was begun in September 1915.   The driving unit was mounted in the fuselage and the propellers were mounted between the wings.   The four 200 H.P. Mercedes engines were fitted one above the other on each side of the fuselage each driving a propeller at 900 r.p.m.   A clear space between the engines made for accessibility and enabled small repairs to be carried out.   Three pressure fuel tanks were fitted in front and behind each engine under the flooring, containing fuel for 6 hours.   The whole driving unit was so arranged that each engine with its gearing, transmission shaft; propeller gearing and propeller formed a complete unit working independently from the other engines.   The trial flights were carried out without any mishap, so that after 12 flights, making a total of 8 hours flight, the military acceptance flight was carried out on Oct. 19th. 1916.   For this flight the weight empty was 6,800 Kg. the useful load 2600 Kg. making a total of 9400 Kg., bringing the wing loading up to 51.7 Kg. per sq.m. and the load per H.P. to 10.7 Kg.   With this load during the acceptance flights the machine climbed to 1000 m. in 10 minutes, 2000 m. in 25 minutes and 3300 m, in 53 minutes.   After a flight of 2. hours the machine made a good landing on the parade ground at Doberitz.   The maximum speed amounted to 130 km. an hour.

      During further test flights at Doberitz several breakages of the crankshaft occurred due to the length of the engine as well as to the engine bed.   Stronger engine bearers properly braced by means of struts were immediately fitted.   The transmission shafts were fitted with universal joints, in order to avoid the rocking movement which so often occurs at the joints. After these alterations had been carried out the machine carried out a 2 hour flight from the workshop at the end of March, 1917, which proved successful and showed the machine to be suitable for active service.   On April 30th the machine was sent to Altauz, on the Eastern front, making a non-stop flight to Konigsberg in 3 hrs. 55 mins.   The great number of flights carried out at the front with this machine always proved the climb and manoeuvrability of the machine to be excellent.   The Army authorities then ordered 6 giant 1040 H.P. D.F.W. machines.

      Reports received from the front showed that even with only two engines running the machine could still be successfully flown.   Early in 1917 the construction of the 6 giant machines type R.II, was begun.   They were fitted with six 260 H.P. Mercedes engines, the arrangements of the engines and propellers being the same as those on R.I.   It was necessary considerably to increase the dimensions of the machines as a useful load of 3400 Kg. was required and therefore the total weight was increased correspondingly.   The first trial flights of the first machine of this series were carried out satisfactorily at the end of August in spite of some slight difficulties.   Special difficulties were encountered with the gearing of the transmission shafts, these shafts revolving at 3000 r.m.p. and therefore giving rise to pronounced vibrations.   The shafts were then enclosed in tubing in order to damp out the vibrations.   The weight empty of this machine was 8600 Kg. and the total weight loaded about 12000 Kg. bringing the load per H.P. up to 11.5 Kg. and the wing loading up to 45 Kg. per sq.m.   In April 1918 the first machine R.15/16 was conveyed to Cologne where its practical value was proved by the great number of flights carried out.   It was then possible to say that the ever-increasing difficulty of the gearing, had been solved satisfactorily in the case of D.F.W. aeroplanes.

DESCRIPTION OF THE 1000 H.P. D.F.W. GIANT MACHINE.
TYPE 2611.

      This machine is fitted with four 260 H.P. engines.   7 petrol tanks are fitted under the flooring in front and behind the engines, containing 2700 litres sufficient for a 7 hour flight.   The petrol is supplied to the carburettors by means of pumps.   The petrol system has been so arranged that any engine can be supplied from any of the tanks, should the tank normally supplying an engine, spring a leak.   A gravity petrol tank containing 150 litres is fitted on the back of the fuselage, from which the engines can be supplied direct, should a breakdown of the petrol system occur.   The gravity tank can be filled by means of an "Allwoiler" pump from the engine room.

www.ingramcontent.com/pod-product-compliance
Lightning Source LLC
Chambersburg PA
CBHW081543090426
42741CB00014BA/3255